Why Do We Sleep

Text by Cathy Evans and Ziggy Hanaor
Illustrations by Polya Plavinskaia

British Library Cataloguing-in-Publication Data.

A CIP record for this book is available from the British Library

ISBN: 978-1-80066-058-8

First published in the UK in 2025, in the US in 2026.

Cicada Books Ltd
Unit 9, Cliff Road Studios
5 Cliff Road
London, NW5 1UE
www.cicadabooks.co.uk

Printed in Poland on FSC® certified paper

MIX
Paper | Supporting responsible forestry
FSC® C163799
www.fsc.org

THIS BOOK BELONGS TO:

_____

_____

_____

_____

Hi there! As you read, see how many sheep you can count throughout the book. I'm number one!

Cathy Evans

Polya Plavinskaia

Why do we SLEEP?

CONTENTS

WHY DO WE SLEEP?

Sleep is an important part of life. When we sleep, our bodies and our brains have time to repair themselves and reset for the next waking day.

Mammals, birds, reptiles, insects and amphibians all sleep. Sleep has even been observed in animals without proper brains, like jellyfish.

I do have a brain!

Hush! You have a collection of nerves, but that doesn't count as a brain!

Some grazing animals like horses, zebras and elephants sleep standing up, so that they can make a speedy escape if a predator creeps up on them.

Without sleep, we struggle to function. Sleep deprivation impacts everything from short-term memory and energy levels to immune system performance.

HOW DO OUR BODIES KNOW WHEN TO SLEEP?

Our brain contains a biological system that is known as a 'circadian clock'. Over the course of a 24-hour cycle, the clock responds to light and darkness and tells our brains to release hormones that make us alert or drowsy at the correct times. A normally functioning circadian clock looks something like this:

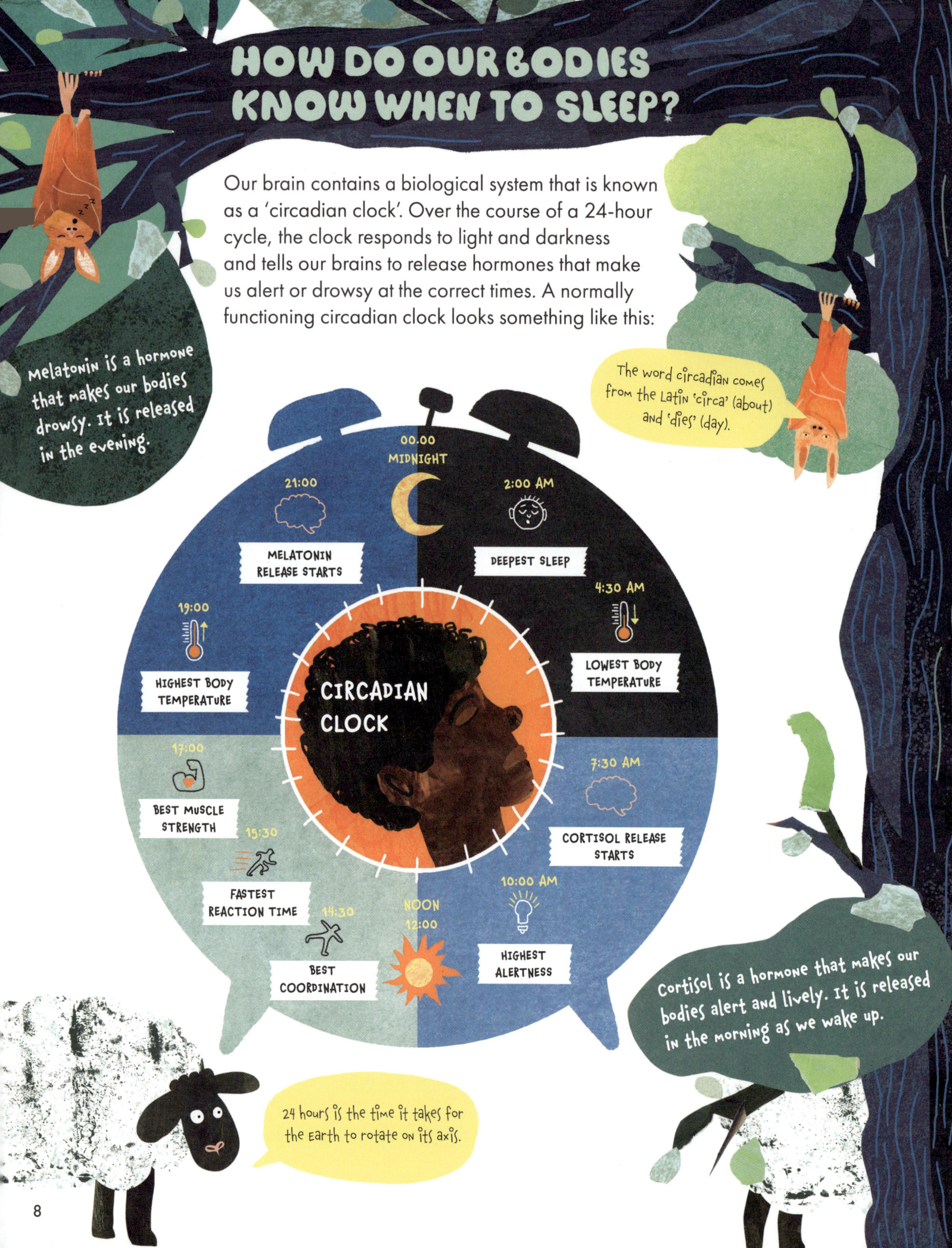

Melatonin is a hormone that makes our bodies drowsy. It is released in the evening.

The word circadian comes from the Latin 'circa' (about) and 'dies' (day).

00.00 MIDNIGHT

21:00
MELATONIN RELEASE STARTS

2:00 AM
DEEPEST SLEEP

19:00
HIGHEST BODY TEMPERATURE

4:30 AM
LOWEST BODY TEMPERATURE

CIRCADIAN CLOCK

17:00
BEST MUSCLE STRENGTH

7:30 AM
CORTISOL RELEASE STARTS

15:30
FASTEST REACTION TIME

14:30
BEST COORDINATION

NOON 12:00

10:00 AM
HIGHEST ALERTNESS

Cortisol is a hormone that makes our bodies alert and lively. It is released in the morning as we wake up.

24 hours is the time it takes for the Earth to rotate on its axis.

All animals (and many plants) on the planet have circadian rhythms. In most animals, sleep hormones are released at night and wakeful hormones are released in the morning. But in nocturnal animals, this is reversed.

WHAT HAPPENS WHEN WE SLEEP?

Every night, the circadian clock in our brain helps our body to go through cycles of sleep. These cycles last around 90 minutes and are repeated four to six times every night. The sleep cycles are made up of two types of sleep: NREM and REM.

NREM

Stands for NON-RAPID EYE MOVEMENT. In this type of sleep, our body functions slow down and our brain is relaxed. We spend about 80% of the night in NREM.

REM

Stands for Rapid Eye Movement. It is a more active type of sleep in which our brain and body are more alert. This is when most of our dreams happen.

There are four stages in every 90 minute sleep cycle:

STAGE 1 (NREM Sleep)

This is the transition from wakefulness to sleep. The brain waves slow down and the muscles relax. This stage only lasts a few minutes.

STAGE 2 (NREM Sleep)

This is the longest stage in the sleep cycle. The body reaches deeper relaxation. Brainwaves slow down, as does the heart rate. The body temperature drops. Occasional spikes of brain activity occur. These are called sleep spindles and scientists don't know what purpose they serve.

STAGE 3 (NREM Sleep)

This is the deepest NREM sleep, when our bodies repair themselves. Known as slow-wave sleep (SWS), our heartbeat, breathing and brainwaves are at their lowest levels. It's quite hard to wake up a person in stage three sleep.

STAGE 4 (REM Sleep)

At the end of each cycle is a short stage of REM sleep. Our brain becomes active, our muscles twitch, our heart rate and breathing speed up and our eyes move rapidly back and forth as we dream. Early in the night, this phase only lasts five minutes. Towards morning, the periods of REM grow longer.

you don't get as much REM sleep in colder climates because your body cannot regulate its temperature properly in REM.

WHY DO WE DREAM?

Scientists are still not sure exactly what dreams are for, but most agree that dreams serve an important role in processing memories and emotions.

Every night, you spend a total of about two hours dreaming, but each dream only lasts between five and 20 minutes. They happen throughout the night but they are most vivid during REM sleep.

NEOCORTEX

BASAL GANGLIA

THALAMUS

HYPOTHALAMUS

AMYGDALA

HIPPOCAMPUS

CEREBELLUM

It is thought that the main purpose of dreams is to process experiences and emotions in a safe, calm environment. The amygdala is a part of your brain that responds to emotions, and it is particularly active during REM sleep.

REM is the only time that the brain stops generating a stress hormone called noradrenaline. In its absence, the brain can revisit some of the trickier feelings that we experienced during the day.

When we dream, the hippocampus transfers memories of the day's events to the neocortex. The neocortex then determines whether to store the information as short-term memory, long-term memory or discard it entirely. This process clears the hippocampus, so that it may function effectively the following day.

Dreams also play a role in organising and storing our daily experiences in memory. The hippocampus, which manages memory, and the neocortex, which handles complex thinking, are two areas of the brain that are very active during sleep.

MEMORY STORAGE

LONG SHORT
LONG SHORT
LONG SHORT

BIN

The scientific study of dreams is called oneirology.

WHAT ARE NIGHTMARES?

Dreams serve another purpose as well; to problem solve. Dreaming can provide us with a 'virtual reality' model of the world, in which we can explore our responses to situations in preparation for the day ahead.

When we have a lot going on at home and at school, we sometimes rehearse the worst-case scenarios in our dreams, leading to vivid nightmares.

Why is that dream in black and white?

Most people dream in colour, but 12% of people dream in black and white.

left handed people may have more vivid dreams than right handed people.

Experiments have shown that REM sleep performs an important role in analysis and learning. When we dream, the parts of our brain associated with logic and social acceptability are less active than the parts of our brain associated with images, memories and emotions. By thinking about a problem in a less logical, less inhibited way, we are sometimes able to come up with a creative solution outside our normal thought patterns.

Many famous artists, scientists and writers say that their best work came to them in a dream. The periodic table, the structure of DNA and some of the best Beatles' songs were all conceived in dreams!

yesterday...All my troubles seemed so far away... YES That's IT!

people who are blind from birth dream NON-VISUAL dreams using other senses.

DO DREAMS HAVE MEANING?

In many ancient civilisations, dreaming was considered a way of receiving messages from the gods. The Ancient Egyptians had trained dreamers, who would help plan battles and make important decisions. The Ancient Greeks believed that dreams allowed the dead to pass messages to the living.

So should we attack from the East or the West?

Er... the West...?

In the 1890s, Sigmund Freud, the founder of psychoanalysis, wrote that dreams offer us a glimpse into the subconscious mind. This is the part of the mind that you are not directly aware of, but which operates in the background, influencing your thoughts, feelings and decisions.

Many psychologists and analysts have expanded on Freud's ideas, exploring how dreams can provide meaningful insights into our deepest unresolved emotions. On the other hand, many behavioural scientists argue that dreams are simply the brain's way of clearing excess information to prevent overload.

I believe that dreams come from desires and thoughts that we push away from our conscious mind, so they don't interfere with daily life.

I desire to go to sleep now.

The truth may lie somewhere in between; dreams likely fulfill a crucial biological purpose while also offering an insight into the thoughts and feelings that we are afraid to look at directly.

INTERPRETATIONS OF SOME COMMON DREAMS

✳ sitting an exam that you have not studied for

This dream often signifies feelings of stress, or a lack of confidence in facing a challenge in your waking life you might feel unprepared for.

Losing your teeth

Dreaming about losing teeth can have many meanings, including feelings of anxiety, insecurity or loss. It can also indicate a need for change.

Finding a new room in your home

This might indicate excitement and anticipation at new opportunities that are being offered to you.

Falling

This dream is most common in the first stages of sleep, when we often have a spasm in our muscles, jerking us awake. This dream might be related to a need to stay alert.

Flying

This is usually a positive dream that boosts confidence in your abilities. However, if the dream is about losing control of your flight, that might relate to losing control in the real world.

Finding yourself naked in a public place

This might mean that you feel vulnerable or that some part of you is open to ridicule and disgrace.

95% of dreams are forgotten within five minutes of waking up, so keep a pad and pen by your bed to jot them down while they're fresh.

When you read the dream back, try to connect not to the events of it, but the to feelings that the dream evoked. Then think about what recent events have triggered a similar emotional response and see if there is a connection between the dream and the event.

HOW DOES THE BODY BENEFIT FROM SLEEP?

It's not just the brain that benefits from sleep.
The rest of the body also uses this time to repair itself.

Heart:

Your heartbeat slows down during sleep and your blood pressure drops. Bad sleepers are known to be more prone to heart disease.

Muscles:

Your body uses the downtime to repair muscles, organs and cells.

Kidneys:

Your kidneys slow down when you sleep, producing less urine, so you don't have to pee very often in the night.

Digestive System:

Lack of sleep causes your body to conserve energy. When you're overly tired, your body produces more hunger hormones, increasing your craving for sweet and salty foods. Sleep deprivation can contribute to weight gain and increase the risk of developing diabetes.

Immune System:

Your immune system is strengthened by sleep. Sleep deprivation can make you more prone to illness.

Skin:

Collagen is a protein that repairs the skin. It is released when we sleep, healing our cuts and bruises.

Bones:

When children sleep, hormones are released, helping their bones to grow.

HOW DO DIFFERENT PEOPLE SLEEP?

All around the world, people have different habits and rituals around sleeping.

In Scandinavian countries like Norway and Sweden, parents often leave their babies outdoors to nap – even in the middle of winter – believing this helps the baby develop a strong immune system.

In warm countries in the Mediterranean, people take a nap in the middle of the day, when it's hottest. In Spain, this is called a *siesta*. In Italy, it's called a *riposo*.

The amount of sleep a child needs per day depends on their age. These are recommended amounts of sleep:

Birth to 3 months: 14 to 17 hours

4 to 12 months: 12 to 16 hours including naps

1 to 2 years: 11 to 14 hours including naps

In Japan, falling asleep at your desk is thought to indicate that you have been working so hard that you've exhausted yourself. Some Japanese companies even provide space for their workers to nap.

Let us worry about you tonight!

Worry dolls are tiny, handcrafted figures. In Central and South America, people share their worries with these dolls, placing them under their pillows at night so that the dolls can take away their anxieties as they sleep.

3 to 5 years:
10 to 13 hours
including naps

6 to 12 years:
9 to 12 hours

13 to 18 years:
8 to 10 hours

Adults:
7 to 9 hours

WHAT IS INSOMNIA?

Everyone has different sleep habits and needs. Some people wake up early, some wake up late and some people simply need less sleep than most.

Most people experience trouble sleeping occasionally, but when sleep is constantly disrupted it is considered a sleep disorder.

Insomnia is a word for troubled sleeping habits. There are three types of insomnia:

Initial insomnia

means you have trouble falling asleep.

Middle insomnia

means you wake up in the middle of the night and struggle to go back to sleep.

Early waking insomnia

is when you wake up too early in the morning and can't get back to sleep.

Women are more likely to experience sleep problems than men.

There are many things that can cause insomnia:

Genetics

If there is a family history of insomnia, you will be more likely to suffer from it.

Medical conditions

Both minor and major illnesses can affect your circadian rhythms.

Mental health

Anxiety or depression can trigger insomnia.

Stress

Stressful situations at home, work or school and major life changes are common causes of insomnia.

Bad habits

Excessive stimulation from screens or caffeine can disrupt sleep (see p. 42).

About half of adults over the age of 65 experience sleep problems.

Insomnia can drain your energy and affect your mood, impacting on your health, memory, decision-making and quality of life.

WHAT ARE SOME OTHER SLEEPING DISORDERS?*

Insomnia is a general disorder but there are other, more specifc, sleep problems that people can suffer from.

sleep-related breathing disorders:

Sleep apnea is a condition in which breathing repeatedly stops and starts during sleep. The most common form, obstructive sleep apnea, happens when the throat muscles become too relaxed, causing the airways to close during inhalation. Loud snoring or waking up gasping for air at night could be signs of sleep apnea.

Circadian rhythm sleep-wake disorders:

When people travel across time zones or work night shifts, their bodies can fall out of sync with a normal 24-hour sleep cycle. This disrupts the release of hormones that regulate wakefulness and drowsiness, causing them to feel sleepy or alert at unusual times and adopt irregular sleep patterns.

One sheep, two sheep, three sheep, four sheep... ...thirty sheep, thirty-one sheep, thirty-two sheep...

Narcolepsy:

Narcolepsy is a condition in which your brain can't control your ability to stay awake. Narcoleptics fall asleep at random points throughout the day. This can cause problems in their daily lives and be difficult to cope with emotionally.

Restless leg syndrome:

This is a condition in which sufferers have an uncomfortable creeping sensation in their feet, calves and thighs, which is relieved when they move around. The symptoms are usually worse at night, so people with this syndrome get up and move around a lot, disrupting their sleep.

REM sleep behaviour disorder:

During REM sleep, the brain temporarily paralyses the body to prevent muscle movement; a state known as atonia. If the brain fails to shut down muscle activity, individuals may act out their dreams by laughing, talking, or abruptly flailing their limbs, waking themselves up.

REM sleep disorders are most common in men over 50.

27

IS IT NORMAL TO SLEEPWALK?

Sleepwalking and talking can be symptoms of a REM sleep behaviour disorder, but if they don't happen frequently, they are nothing to worry about.

sleep-talking

Also called somniloquy, sleep-talking can happen at any stage in the sleep cycle. Sleep-talking can range from mumbling sounds to loud shouts or clear sentences.

sleepwalking

Also known as somnambulism, sleepwalking usually happens within the first few hours of the night, in deep NREM stage sleep. The sleepwalker's eyes may be open, but they are not conscious and will look right through you if you try to talk to them.

Sleepwalkers have been known to walk about, eat, open cupboards and even cook or drive cars — dangerous activities to do whilst sleeping!

No no no!.. Pass me the crocodile... I need to put it in a burrito...

28

If you find someone sleepwalking, the best thing to do is to guide them back to bed and speak in calm, reassuring tones. Do not startle the person or shout at them, as they may lash out unexpectedly. Most sleepwalking episodes last ten minutes or less and the sleepwalker usually has no memory of it in the morning.

Sleepwalking can start at any age but it is most common in children. Sleepwalking can be made worse in times of stress or illness. It is genetic, so if someone is a sleepwalker in your family, you have more of a chance of becoming a sleepwalker too!

WHAT ARE NIGHT TERRORS?

Night terrors are a childhood condition that is different to nightmares. The child partly wakes up and the area of the brain that controls 'fight-or-flight' responses becomes overactive, leading to a panic response.

NIGHT TERRORS

* MOSTLY AFFECT CHILDREN AGES 3-8.
* HAPPEN IN NREM DEEP SLEEP STAGE.
* USUALLY OCCUR EARLY IN THE NIGHT, WITHIN 2-3 HOURS OF FALLING ASLEEP.
* ARE OFTEN ACCOMPANIED BY THRASHING AND SCREAMING.
* CAN'T BE REMEMBERED AFTERWARDS.

NIGHTMARES

* AFFECT BOTH CHILDREN AND ADULTS.
* HAPPEN IN REM SLEEP.
* USUALLY OCCUR LATER IN THE NIGHT.
* ARE GENERALLY NOT ACTED OUT.
* CAN SOMETIMES BE REMEMBERED AFTERWARDS.

HOW CAN I HELP SOMEONE WITH NIGHT TERRORS?

Stay calm and do not try to wake them up unless there's a chance they could hurt themselves.

If they're having a night terror at the same time every night, try waking them up 15 minutes beforehand every night for a week. This can sometimes stop the night terrors happening.

Try having a relaxing bedtime routine and talk openly about things that might be causing stress or anxiety.

Night terrors usually go away on their own before the teenage years.

HOW DO ANIMALS SLEEP?

Swifts

These birds eat, drink and sleep on the wing. They can spend seven months of the year in flight, only landing during nesting season.

Bees

Bees sometimes fall asleep inside the head of a flower.

Cats

Cats are fabulous sleepers. A house cat sleeps for 13-16 hours a day and a lion can sleep for 20 hours a day!

Great apes

Apes build sleeping platforms in trees so that they can sleep comfortably and safely. This means they can get long periods of sleep, which is important for brain development.

Bats

We all know that bats sleep upside down, but do you know why? It's because their wings aren't strong enough to take off from the ground. They need to stay elevated at all times so they can drop into flight from their perches.

Giraffes

Giraffes need the least amount of sleep of any mammal. They only sleep for 30 minutes a day, usually in five-minute bursts.

Otters

Otters sleep in groups, holding hands so that they don't drift away from each other. They float on their backs and sometimes anchor themselves by wrapping seaweed around their bodies.

Orcas

Orca babies and mothers don't sleep at all for the first month after birth. This is because the baby orca doesn't have enough blubber to stay warm and afloat, so it needs to stay in its mother's slipstream. The mother needs to stay awake to make sure the baby doesn't go astray.

Walruses

Walruses can go 84 hours without sleep, but when they do drift off, they can sleep for up to 19 hours without waking.

Dolphins

Dolphins must keep moving to regulate their body temperature, so they experience unihemispheric sleep; a type of sleep where only one half of the brain rests at a time. They keep one eye open to avoid bumping into things.

Many migratory birds such as ducks and frigatebirds also experience unihemispheric sleep.

Sperm whales

Sperm whales sleep vertically for short periods, bobbing up and down like corks.

DO ANIMALS DREAM?

Anyone with a dog or a cat knows that when their pet sleeps, they seem to be dreaming. They make little sounds, their breathing becomes irregular and their legs twitch as though they are running.

REM is experienced by all mammals and all birds, in some reptiles and in a handful of other animals, including spiders, crabs and cuttlefish.

Birds and reptiles experience REM in short bursts of a few seconds up to 350 times a night. Mammals, on the other hand, have much longer periods of REM sleep, allowing time for more vivid dreams. There is also variation within mammals. Big dogs dream for longer than small dogs, for example.

In one experiment, researchers scanned the brain of a sleeping rat after it ran a maze and observed that the neurons related to navigation were activated. This suggests that, like humans, rats likely use dreams to process memories and solve problems. Studies have also shown that animals deprived of REM sleep exhibit confusion, irritability and slowed brain activity—similar to the effects seen in humans.

Humans rely heavily on their sense of sight, which is why our dreams are rich with visual imagery. However, animals like dogs or mice, which depend more on their sense of smell, may dream in very different ways.

What animals dream about we'll never know for certain, but it seems that their dreams are as chaotic and confusing as ours, and similar to us, they draw on daytime experiences, helping the brain to make sense of reality. As with humans, much of animal dreaming remains a mystery.

WHAT IS HIBERNATION?*

As the winter sets in, many animals struggle to find food. Without food, they must conserve their energy and so they go into a deep sleep-like state called hibernation.

Hibernating means different things in different animals. A chipmunk will enter into a state of temporary hibernation called torpor, waking up every week or so to feed on nuts and seeds stored away in warmer months. A dormouse, on the other hand, will not wake up for up to 11 months at a time!

DORMOUSE

HEDGEHOG

COMMON TOAD

CHIPMUNK

TORTOISE

The state of hibernation is different to that of sleep. When a hedgehog sleeps in the summer months, its body temperature will drop to around 30°C and its breathing will slow but remain steady. During hibernation, its body temperature drops to around 8°C and it can go two hours without drawing a single breath!

Throughout the winter months, a bear will lose up to 40% of its body weight.

BEARS

Hibernation is common among small mammals, as their bodies can quickly adjust temperature. Most large animals don't hibernate, as their bodies take too long to cool down and warm up. Bears are the exception. To prepare for their extended rest, bears eat lots of high-energy food, building up fat reserves and growing an extra-thick coat of fur. They then retreat to a den and enter a state of light hibernation known as denning. During this time, their body temperature drops only slightly and they can be awakened relatively easily. Amazingly, many female bears give birth and suckle their young whilst denning.

SLEEP MYTHS

There is so much mystery surrounding sleep and dreams that it is not surprising that many theories have found their way into religions and mythologies around the world.

HYPNOS

Hypnos is the god of sleep in Ancient Greek mythology. He is the brother of Thanatos (Death) and the son of Nyx (Night). A calm and gentle god, Hypnos lives in the underworld in a cave where no light or sound can ever reach. His son is Morpheus, the god of dreams.

THE SANDMAN

This is a mythical character from European folklore. He sprinkles magical sand onto sleepers' eyes to encourage both good and bad dreams. The grit in your eyes when you wake up is the leftover sand.

Fylgja

This is a female guardian spirit from Norse mythology, who appears in dreams to warn you about future dangers. She can appear as a beautiful woman or she can appear as a wolf, bear or other creature that relates to your personality. If she is seen during a person's waking hours, it is an omen of death.

The Baku

This Japanese mythological creature is made up of all the bits left over when the gods had finished creating the world's animals. He has the head of an elephant, the body of a bear, the eyes of a rhino and the feet of a tiger. The baku wanders around at night and feasts on people's nightmares. If you wake up from a bad dream, you can call the baku and he will eat it up. But be careful not to call the baku too often or he might eat your dreams and hopes as well as your nightmares!

Dream Catchers

Dream catchers have their origins in the Anishinabek indigenous cultures of North America. According to legend, a grandmother noticed a spider weaving its web near her bed. When her grandchild tried to kill the spider, she rescued it. In gratitude, the spider gifted her a magical dream-catching web that trapped nightmares but allowed good dreams to pass through. Dream catchers are common amongst other indigenous cultures across North America and are used to shield children from bad dreams and illness.

41

HOW CAN WE SLEEP BETTER?

'Sleep hygiene' is the term used to describe the habits and environments that play a role in how well you sleep. By improving our sleep hygiene we can benefit from a more restful night.

Create a comfortable sleep environment

Make sure your bedroom is cool, quiet, dark and well-ventilated. You might want to use blackout curtains, earplugs or 'white noise' to reduce stimulation.

Minimise stress

If you worry at night, you could write down the things that are causing you anxiety before you go to bed, giving yourself permission to let them go until the morning.

Establish a regular routine

In the hour before bedtime, have a bath, read for 20 minutes, listen to soothing music or meditate. When you have a routine, your brain knows that it's time to start winding down.

Minimise screen-time around bedtime

Avoid televisions, computers and phones in the two hours before bed. Blue light, which is emitted from such devices, has been shown to disrupt circadian rhythms. Avoid using screens in the bedroom generally. The bedroom should be a place of relaxation and not stimulation.

Lead a healthy lifestyle

Exercise regularly, eat well, avoid heavy meals before bedtime and try not to nap throughout the day.

WHAT TYPE OF SLEEPER ARE YOU?

Chronotypes are the natural preferences of the body for wakefulness and sleep. Some people are early birds and others are night owls. Whilst circadian rhythms can be adjusted, chronotypes are usually genetic and are harder to adjust.

Bear

A bear chronotype is in tune with the rhythms of the planet. Bears typically go to bed around 11 pm and wake up around 7 am. They are most productive between 10 and 2.

Wolf

Wolf chronotypes are night owls. They go to bed very late and will happily sleep until noon. They are most energetic from around 1 till 5 pm. Don't try waking a wolf early unless you want a snap!

Lion

Lion chronotypes are early birds. They go to bed early, wake up early, and are productive from around 9 am till 1 pm. They get tired at the end of the day and struggle to maintain social arrangements in the evening.

Dolphin

Dolphins sleep with one eye open and the dolphin chronotype has trouble following any sleep schedule. Insomniacs are dolphins, struggling to fall asleep or stay asleep and often waking early in the morning.

10%

55%

15%

15%

Bears are the most common chronotype and dolphins the least common.

Most people fall somewhere in between these four chronotypes. Chronotype can also change as a person ages. Children tend to have early 'lion' chronotypes, whilst teenagers often have a later 'wolf' chronotype.

Some researchers think that chronotypes might have been a survival technique that evolved when humans were hunter-gatherers. By taking turns sleeping there was always someone awake to keep watch.

THE SLEEP FLOW CHART

Feeling persistently tired? Journey through this flow diagram to work out how to improve your sleep quality.

START HERE

Is your room a comfortable temperature for sleeping?

········ **NO** ········ The ideal temperature for sleeping is 16 – 20°c. Think about adding or reducing blankets to achieve the right temperature.

YES

Is it dark enough?

········ **NO** ········ Light can make us feel alert and disrupt sleep. Blackout blinds or an eye mask can lead to a more restful night.

YES

Is it quiet and undistracted by noise?

········ **NO** ········ If noise keeps you awake, consider using earplugs or white noise.

YES

Do you avoid caffeine in the 8 hours before sleeping?

········ **NO** ········ As much as possible, steer clear of energy drinks, coffee, and other stimulants in the afternoon and evening.

YES

do you eat your main meal more than two hours before bedtime?

· · · · NO · · · · Avoid heavy foods before bed so that your body isn't digesting as you sleep.

YES

do you exercise regularly?

· · · · NO · · · · Exercise during the day releases endorphins, hormones that relieve stress, aid wellbeing and help sleep.

YES

Do you use a phone or tablet in the hours before bedtime?

· · · · YES · · · · Avoid using devices at least an hour before bedtime. Leave them outside your room if possible!

NO

Do you have the same routine before bedtime every night?

· · · · NO · · · · Having the same nightly wind-down routine helps your brain prepare itself for sleep.

YES

Well done! you should sleep like a baby!

If you've made these changes and are still struggling with tiredness and poor sleep after two weeks, try talking to a trusted adult or your doctor.

GLOSSARY

Atonia
A temporary state of muscle paralysis that occurs during REM so that the dreamer does not enact their dreams as they sleep.

Chronotype
A person's natural tendency to sleep and wake at certain times. It's also known as diurnal preference.

Circadian rhythm
The 24-hour cycle of physical, mental and behavioral changes that occur in an organism. It's controlled by a small part of the brain that responds to light and dark.

Cortisol
Also known as the stress hormone, cortisol regulates your sleep-wake cycle by helping you wake up and stay awake. It is at its highest levels in the early morning and at its lowest in the evening.

Hibernation
During hibernation, an animal's heart rate and breathing slow right down. Their body temperature also decreases. These changes help hibernating animals survive using less energy during the cold winter months when food is scarce.

Insomnia
A sleep disorder that makes it hard to fall asleep, stay asleep, or get quality sleep. It can also cause you to wake up too early and not be able to get back to sleep.

Melatonin
A hormone that helps regulate your sleep-wake cycle and circadian rhythm. The pineal gland in your brain produces melatonin in response to darkness. In the hour before bed, your melatonin levels increase.

Narcolepsy
A rare long-term condition in which the brain is unable to regulate sleeping, meaning that the person will suddenly fall asleep during the day.

Night terrors
A childhood condition that causes a person to wake up suddenly in a state of intense fear; often screaming and thrashing around. Night terrors usually happen in the first hours of sleep.

NREM
Non-rapid eye movement (NREM) sleep is a restful phase of sleep when a person's brain activity, breathing, and heart rate slow down.

Oneirology
The scientific study of dreams and how they relate to the brain's functions.

REM

Rapid eye movement (REM) sleep is a stage of sleep when your eyes move rapidly while closed, and you experience most of your dreams. Your brain is most active at this stage of the sleep cycle.

sleep apnea

A sleep disorder that causes breathing to repeatedly stop and start during sleep.

sleep cycles

Every night a person goes through four to six sleep cycles, each lasting around 90 minutes. These cycles are made up of three stages of NREM sleep followed by a shorter stage of lighter REM sleep. The sleep cycles help regulate body and brain functions.

sleep hygiene

A set of habits and environmental factors that can help you sleep better.

sleep spindles

Bursts of brain activity that occur during NREM sleep. Whilst we still don't know exactly what purpose they serve, they are linked to memory processing, brain development and sensory processing.

slow-wave sleep

The deepest stage of non-rapid eye movement (NREM) sleep. It's also known as deep sleep and it occurs in stage three of the sleep cycle.

Somnambulism

Also known as sleepwalking, this is a sleep disorder in which the sleeping person gets up, walks around and sometimes performs complex functions whilst still asleep. It usually happens in the early hours of the night and it is best to calmly guide the sleepwalker back to bed without waking them up.

Somniloquy

Also known as sleep-talking, this is when someone speaks in their sleep, either in words or gibberish, without being aware of it.

Torpor

A lighter form of hibernation. An animal's body temperature and heart rate drop, allowing it to conserve energy through the winter. It will, however, wake up at intervals to eat food stashed away during the summer months.

unihemispheric sleep

A sleep state in which one half of the brain is asleep while the other half is awake. It is common in birds and sea mammals that are in constant motion, preventing them from crashing into things.

I'm the last sheep in the book! Including me, there are 55. Did you find all of us?